The Heavenly Cookbook:

The Legacy of Mrs. Ida Mae Riley-Sylvester

By Corlisa Warren Spurlock

The Heavenly Cookbook:

The Legacy of Mrs. Ida Mae Riley-Sylvester

Copyright © 2023 Corlisa Warren-Spurlock

ISBN: 978-1-956884-19-7

Contributing Editor: All services completed by Imprint Productions, Inc.
Cover Design: All services completed by Imprint Productions, Inc.

Printed in the United States of America Published by Imprint Productions, Inc.
First Edition 2023

Contact: **info@imprintproductionsinc.com**

Visit Us: **www.imprintproductionsinc.com**

Acknowledgements

God the Father, my beginning and end, thank you for giving me the courage, strengthening me when doubts came upon me, and guiding me to lean on your understanding and not my own. It's with great appreciation and gratitude that I would like to acknowledge those who supported me. I would not be who I am today without the steady hands and unconditional love of my deceased parents. Both parents supported me during my careers. My Georgia Peach Hubby, Arrie, my love, friend, partner, and soulmate. My darling daughter Dr. Regina Boateng, most loving and adorable woman. Thank you for your help and guidance. My forever missed son, the late Julitine Emmanuel Nelson, gone but not forgotten. Thank you to all the amazing women and men in my life who have kept me lifted in prayer. You all know who you are and what you mean to me. My girlfriends, mentors and all of you who have supported me during this writing process. You have helped me become a better woman. I also want to thank my Pastor, Timothy McBride, Co-Pastor, Shunnae McBride, the Ministers of the Gospel, and my Life Coach for encouraging me. Finally, I would like to thank Dr. Brunetta Nelson and the Imprint Productions, Inc. team for their work.

Dedication

My Dear Mother: Ida Mae Riley-Sylvester I wrote this story for you. When I began writing it, I had not realized how saddened I would be after you had transitioned. I remember, you would always start your cooking around 5:00 a.m. Your amazing cooking was SOOO good for family and friends that it would last sometimes for three days. By the time this book is released you will be rejoicing in Heaven on your 85th Birthday, and we will be celebrating your legacy through your cooking! As you would say, "If I couldn't do anything else for you, I can surely feed you. I do not like to see anyone going around hungry." Mother Ida, I would much prefer it, if you were alive and well. My love for you shall live forever. You will always be in my heart, and my mind.

Your hands made all your cooking recipes with love. Your vegetables were home grown. You loved canning, planting, and harvesting food for your family gatherings and church events. You were well known for your favorite dessert dish PEACH COBBLER. "RIP MOTHER IDA" Gone but not forgotten.

WITH MUCH LOVE,

Corlisa

Isaiah 54:17

No weapon that is formed against thee
shall prosper and every tongue that shall rise against
thee in judgment thou shall condemn. This is the
heritage of the servants of the Lord, and their
righteousness is of me, saith the Lord.

A Message from Mrs. Ida Sylvester

I dedicate this book to my family and friends. Down through the years, we have enjoyed many gatherings filled with laughter and love. Cooking is my heart! It has been a pleasure sharing my gift and passion with you. This book contains various recipes prepared and shared with many. Whether you are cooking for family, church gathering, or community event, don't forget to add the most important ingredients: a dash of love and a sprinkle of faith (for those of us who are culinarily challenged)! May you eat until you want no more. Be Blessed!

-   From Mother Ida, before her transition.

Table of Contents

Mother Ida Used to Say...

"It's the Glory of God, how I made it overcome."

BAKED CHICKEN, GREEN BEAN & SQUASH CASSEROLES

What You'll Need:

- 30 oz Worcestershire Sauce
- Flour
- Paprika
- Pepper
- Salt
- 2 Eggs Beaten
- ¾ Cups of Milk
- ¼ Cup Melted Butter
- 1 Pack of Buttery Crackers
- Your Choice of Other Seasonings
- Chicken Breast with Skin
- 4 Cans Whole Green Beans
- 1 Cup 8 oz Sour Cream
- 1 Can Mushroom Soup
- 1 Can French Onions
- 4 Cups Sliced Yellow Squash
- ¼ Cup Chopped Onions
- 1 Cup Shredded Cheese

What to Do:
1. Mix a cup of water with 30 oz of Worcestershire sauce.
2. Pour the mixture into a pan.
3. Wash and season your chicken.
4. Place the chicken into the pan and spread the sauce over the chicken, skin side up.
5. Cover the pan with foil and bake the chicken in the oven at 350 degrees, for 30 to 35 minutes.
6. Uncover the chicken to let it brown in the oven.

While the Chicken Bakes, Start Your Green Beans & Squash:
1. Mix the mushroom soup and the sour cream together.
2. Pour the mixture over the green beans.
3. Cook the green beans until they are bubbling, then top with French onions.
4. Bake at 350 degrees for 5-10 minutes or until browned.

Yellow Squash Casserole:
1. Place squash and onions in a large skillet over medium heat and add a bit of water.
2. Cover and cook for about 5 minutes, until squash is tender. Drain and place into a large bowl.
3. In a medium bowl, mix cracker crumbs and cheese.
4. Stir half the cracker mixture into the cooked squash and onions.
5. In a small bowl, mix the eggs and milk, then add the squash mixture.
6. Bake at 350 degrees for 10 minutes or until browned.

How sweet it is to be loved by this healthy serving. This one is finger licking good. This one is a healthy choice.

Mother Ida Used to Say...
"Without a doubt, God will provide."

Mother Ida Mae Riley-Sylvester

Ribs, Dressing, and Green Beans Good Gosh Oh Molly!

What You'll Need:

- 1 Slab of Ribs
- Meat Tenderizer
- Season All or Your Choice of Seasoning
- 2 Cups of Hoover Medium Meal
- ½ Cup of Self-rising Flour
- 1 Cup of Milk
- 1 White Onion
- 1 Green Bell Pepper

- 4 Celery Stalks
- 5 Beaten Eggs
- 1lb Chicken Necks
- 1 32oz Can of Chicken Stock
- 1 Cup of Water
- 3 oz Worcestershire Sauce
- Salt
- Pepper

What to Do:

1. Mix a cup of water with 3oz of Worcestershire sauce and pour it into a pan.
2. Add Season all or your choice of seasoning.
3. Spread the mixture over the ribs and cover the pan for 45 minutes until the ribs are tender.
4. Uncover it so it can be tenderly heated at 355 degrees.
5. Pour your favorite barbecue sauce over the ribs.

That Good Ole Fashioned Turkey Dressing:

1. Boil chicken necks and chicken stock for approximately 15 minutes. Pick meat off the bones.
2. Pre-heat oven to 350 degrees.
3. Mix the remaining ingredients together. Add the chicken.
4. Bake for approximately 30 minutes or less. Don't dry it out!

Look at this display soul food platter homemade dressing, seasoned green beans and those smoked ribs sooo very tasty as you chewing flavors burst into your mouth!

Proverbs 3: 5-8

Trust in the Lord with all thine heart;
and lean not unto thine own understanding. 6. In all
thy ways acknowledge him, and he shall direct thy
paths. 7. Be not wise in thine own eyes: fear the Lord,
and depart from evil. 8. It shall be health to thy navel,
and marrow to thy bones.

Mother Ida Used to Say...
"Without a doubt, God will provide."

OXTAILS

What you need:

- 1 Pack of Oxtails
- Meat Tenderizer
- Oxtail Seasoning
- White Vinegar
- Water

- Yellow Onion
- Green Bell Pepper
- Black Pepper
- Lawry's Season Salt
- Aluminum Foil

What to Do:

1. Soak oxtails in white vinegar and water overnight.
2. Season oxtails with oxtail seasoning, salt, pepper, Lawry's season salt, and meat tenderizer.
3. Place the oxtails with yellow onions and green bell peppers.
4. Boil the oxtails for 2 hours and 15 minutes, at 450 degrees, until tender.

Hmm, hmm, those ox tails are sooo tender and soft. You could eat them without any dentures.

Psalms 91: 2-14

2. I will say of the Lord, He is my refuge and my fortress: my God; in him will I trust. 14. Because he hath set his love upon me, therefore will I deliver him: I will set him on high, because he hath known my name.

Mother Ida Used to Say...
"I put all things in the Master's hands."

Peach Cobbler

What You Need:

- 4 Cans of Peaches
- 2 Cups of Sugar
- 2 Sticks of Butter
- 2 Small Cans of Pineapple Juice
- 1 Cup of Cooking Oil
- 1-2lb Bag of Self-Rising Flour
- 1 Teaspoon of Vanilla Extract

What to Do:

1. Drain the peach juice, saving one cup for later.
2. Cut the peaches into halves.
3. Mix half a cup of the peach juice with melted butter and the other half with a small bit of flour.
4. Heat the juice and butter mixture together and use the flour to thicken up the sauce.
5. Mix the finished sauce with the peaches.
6. Place the peach mixture into your crust and cover with a top crust layer.
7. Bake at 350 degrees until top crust is browned.

Mother Ida's delicious peach cobbler would smack the taste out of your mouth!

Psalm 23: 1-6

1. The Lord is my shepherd; I shall not want. 2. He maketh me to lie down in green pasture; he leadeth me beside the still waters. 3. He restoreth my soul: he leadeth me in the paths of righteousness for his name's sake. 4. Yea, though I walk through the valley of the shadow of death, I will fear no evil: for thou art with me: thy rod and thy staff the comfort me, 5. Thou preparest a table before me in the presence of mine enemies: thou anointest my head with oil; my cup runneth over. 6. Surely goodness and mercy shall follow me all the days of my life: and I will dwell in the house of the Lord forever.

SWEET POTATO PIE

What You Need:

- 2 Cups Mashed Sweet Potatoes
- 3 Eggs
- 1 Unbaked Pie Crust
- 1 ¼ Cups of Sugar
- ¼ Cup of Pineapple Juice
- 1 Stick of Butter
- 2 Teaspoon Vanilla Extract
- ½ Cup Evaporated Milk
- ¼ Teaspoon of Salt

What to Do:

1. Cream potatoes using a blender or a mixer.
2. Combine all the ingredients and pour into the unbaked pie crust.
3. Bake at 425 Degrees for 15 minutes.
4. Bake for 350 for 45 minutes.

Y'all know Mother Ida put her foot in this one! You can't just eat one slice with cool whip. Watch out! Your taste buds will be sooo amazed that you will have a sweet tooth!

May the Work I've Done Speak for Me

"The works I've done,
Sometimes it seems so small,
It seems like I've done nothing at all.
Lord I'm leaning and depending on You,
If I do right, you're gonna see me through;
May the works (the works I've done),
Let it speak for me (for me)"

Proverbs 31: 10-16

10. Who can find a virtuous woman?
For her price is far above rubies. 11. The heart of her
husband doth safely trust in her, so that he shall have
no need of spoil. 12. She will do him good and not evil
all the days of her life. 13. She seeketh wool, and flax,
and worketh willingly with her hands. 14. She is like the
merchants' ships; she bringeth her food from afar. 15.
She riseth also while it is yet right, and giveth meat to
her household, and a portion to her maidens. 16. She
considereth a field, and buyeth it: with the fruit of her
hands she planteth a vineyard.

About the Author

Corlisa Warren-Spurlock is the author of an adult novel native of Florida. The Florida naïve worked as a Public Officer and enjoys Christian service, reading and sharing her writing story. Corlisa is currently retired and hard at work on her first adult novel. More important, it is her ultimate desire to write this book. She can usually be found caring for self-care, communicating with her loved ones or the love her life family, friends or sitting out on the patio with her favorite cup of coffee or tea.

Being Faithful and Grateful is to believe that our journey is all that matters. God's Heaven has been the foundation for happiness and peace. She raised her eyes towards heaven. Heaven knows I've tried to help others, and she has helped me! Feed your Faith and starve your soul of doubts and fears for Victory.

Rest in peace, my

Mother Ida Mae Riley-Sylvester

Mother Ida Used to Say...
"Keep Living!"